FAR

The Book of the Hanging Gardens

and Other Songs

for Voice and Piano

ARNOLD SCHOENBERG

D0339460

DOVER PUBLICATIONS, INC.
New York

Copyright

Copyright © 1995 by Dover Publications, Inc.
All rights reserved under Pan American and International Copyright Conventions.

Bibliographical Note

This Dover edition, first published in 1995, is a new compilation of songs originally published separately. Verlag Dreililien Berlin originally published the following separate collections for voice and piano: *Four Songs, Op. 2* (1904); *Six Songs, Op. 3* (medium voice) (1904); and *Eight Songs, Op. 6* (1905). Universal-Edition A. G. Wien [Vienna] originally published *15 Gedichte aus "Das Buch der hängenden Gärten" von Stefan George für eine Singstimme und Klavier, Op. 15* (1914); and four songs from *Gurrelieder (J. P. Jacobsen) von Arnold Schönberg / Klavierauszug von Alban Berg: Lied Waldemars: "So tanzen die Engel..."* (1914), *Lied Toves: "Nun sag' ich Dir zum ersten Mal..."* (1914), *Lied Waldemars: "Du wunderliche Tove!"* (1914) and *Lied der Waldtaube* (1912). *Six Orchestral Songs, Op. 8, Arranged by Anton Webern,* were originally published in an unidentified edition, n.d.

The Dover edition adds: a composite list of contents in German and English; a glossary of German terms in the music, including footnotes and longer score notes; and new English prose translations of the song texts by Stanley Appelbaum. New German and English headings have been added throughout.

Library of Congress Cataloging-in-Publication Data

Schoenberg, Arnold, 1874–1951.
   [Songs. Selections]
   The book of the hanging gardens : and other songs : for voice and piano / Arnold Schoenberg.
      p.   cm.
   German words; also printed as text with English translation.
   Reprint. Collected from various eds.
   Contents: Four songs, op. 2 — Six songs, op. 3 — Eight songs, op. 6 — Six orchestral songs, op. 8 — Das Buch der hängenden Gärten : op. 15 — Four songs from Gurrelieder.
   ISBN 0-486-28562-6 (pbk.)
   1. Songs with piano. I. Title.
M1620.S364B66   1995   95-14168
                                                                     CIP
                                                                        M

Manufactured in the United States of America
Dover Publications, Inc., 31 East 2nd Street, Mineola, N.Y. 11501

CONTENTS

Das Buch der hängenden Gärten
(The Book of the Hanging Gardens), Op. 15 (1908–9)

Fifteen Songs on Texts of Stefan George

Four Songs from *Gurrelieder (Songs of Gurre)*
(begun *ca.* 1901; completed 1911)

Danish text by Jens Peter Jacobsen; German version by Robert Franz Arnold
Arranged for piano & voice by Alban Berg

GLOSSARY OF GERMAN TERMS

abnehmend, diminishing
ausdrucksvoll, expressively

beschleunigend, accelerating
bewegt, moving, agitated
bewegter, steigernd, increasingly agitated, *crescendo*
(**pp**) *bleiben, aber etwas steigern*, continued **pp**,
   but becoming slightly louder
breit, (pathetisch), broad (with pathos)

drängend, pressing forward
durchaus sehr zart, etwas langsamer, always very subdued,
   somewhat slower

erstes Zeitmaß, Tempo I
etwas belebend, becoming a little livelier
etwas bewegt(er), somewhat more agitated
etwas breit(er), a little broader
etwas drängend, pressing forward a little
etwas flüchtiger, somewhat more fleeting
etwas getragen, kräftig, rather solemn, forceful
etwas langsam(er), somewhat slow(er)
etwas rascher, (leicht), a little quicker, (free)
etwas zögernd, a bit hesitant
etwas zurückhaltend, holding back a little

feurig, fiery, passionate
fließend(er), (more) flowing
flüchtig, fleeting

gedampftes Forte, subdued *forte*
gehend, moving
gleichmaßiges **pp** *ohne* cresc., *sempre* **pp** *senza cresc.*

hervorheben, bring out, emphasize
hervortreten, prominent, to the fore

immer abnehmend, sempre diminuendo
immer steigernd, sempre crescendo
im Zeitmaß, a tempo
innig, expressive, heartfelt
ins erste Zeitmaß, in the first tempo

kräftig, breit, forceful, broad

langsam(e)(er), slow(er)
leicht, free
leicht, aber nicht allzu rasch, free, but not too quick
leicht bewegt, (sehr zart), lightly moving, (very gentle)
l. H. [linke Hand], left hand

mäßig(e), (bewegt), moderate, (moving)
mäßig, innig, moderate, expressive
mit bewegtem Ausdruck, touchingly expressive
mit größter Warme, with great warmth
mit Schwung, spirited
mit zartem Ausdruck, gently expressive

nach und nach steigernd, crescendo poco a poco
nicht beschleunigen (starres Zeitmaß), non accelerando
   (steady tempo)
nicht eilen, without haste
nicht zu langsam, not too slow
nicht zu rasch, not too quick

ohne accel., without speeding up
ohne Pedal, without pedal
ohne rit., without slowing down

rasch(er), quick(er)
rasch, mit verhaltener Heftigkeit, quick, with suppressed
   intensity
rasch steigernd, stringendo
r. H. [rechte Hand], right hand
r. H. übernimmt, the right hand [plays] the upper part
ruhige (Bewegung), calm (motion)
ruhig(er), calm(er)

schwungvoll, spirited
sehr ausdrucksvoll (aber ohne Steigerung), very expressively
   (but without becoming more intense)
sehr breit, very broad
sehr gebunden, molto legato
sehr innig, (mäßig bewegt), very expressive, (moderately
   moving)
sehr langsam, very slow
sehr lebhaft, very lively
sehr rasch (und leicht), very quick (and free)
sehr ruhig, very calm
sehr weich, very delicate, tender
sehr zart, very subdued, gentle
sehr zurückhaltend, very held back
steigernd, (etwas beschleunigend), crescendo (poco accelerando)

verlaufend, dying away
viel langsamer, much slower

warm, (voll), warm, full
weich, delicate, smooth, tender
wieder beruhigend, once more becoming calm
wieder breit, broad again
wieder etwas langsamer, once again somewhat slower
wieder im Zeitmaß, again in tempo
wieder ins Tempo, once more in tempo
wieder langsam(er), slow(er) once again
wieder ruhig, calmer again
wieder wie früher, once again as earlier
wieder wie vorher, once again as before
wie vorher, as before

zart, subdued, gentle
Zeitmaß, tempo
zögernd, hesitant
zurückhaltend, holding back

FOOTNOTES AND LONGER SCORE NOTES

Page 98, 3rd system, tempo marking ("Wenn Vöglein klagen . . . ," Op. 8, No. 6):

♩ = ♪ *von vorher, etwas langsamer*

♩ = the previous ♪, but slower

Page 101, footnote (*Das Buch der hängenden Gärten*, No. I):
Die beigesetzten Metronomzahlen dürfen nicht wörtlich genommen werden, sondern sollen bloß die Zahleinheit (♩ ♩ ♪) des Grundtempos andeuten, aus welchem das Tempo frei zu gestalten ist.

The metronome markings given here need not be followed exactly. They suggest only a general basis for a fundamental tempo that underlies related note values and tempos.

Page 116, footnote (*Das Buch der hängenden Gärten*, No. VIII):
Immer die vorschlagende Sechzehntelnote stärker als den darauffolgenden Akkord.

Play each prefatory sixteenth note louder than the chord that follows it.

Page 117, 3rd & 4th systems (*Das Buch der hängenden Gärten*, No. VIII):
linke Hand immer gleich stark bis zum Schluß

the left hand always equally strong until the end

Page 160, 2nd system (*Lied der Waldtaube*):
(mächtig anschwellend, aber nur sehr wenig beschleunigend)

(with a powerful buildup, but only slightly accelerating)

TRANSLATIONS OF SONG TEXTS

by Stanley Appelbaum

Four Songs
Op. 2 (1899)

1. Erwartung (Expectation)
Poem by Richard Dehmel

Out of the sea-green pond next to the red villa under the dead oak, the moon shines. Where the oak's dark reflection reaches through the water, a man stands and removes a ring from his hand. Three opals gleam; red and green sparks float though the pale stones and die away. And he kisses them, and his eyes glow like the sea-green bottom of the pond: a window opens. Out of the red villa next to the dead oak a pale woman's hand beckons to him . . .

2. Schenk mir deinen goldenen Kamm (Give me your golden comb)
Poem by Richard Dehmel

(Jesus begs)
Give me your golden comb; every morning shall remind you that you kissed my hair. Give me your silken sponge; every evening I want to sense for whom you are preparing yourself in your bath, oh, Mary, oh, Mary! Give me everything you have; my soul has no vanity, proudly I shall receive your blessing. Give me your heavy burden: won't you also lay your heart, your heart, upon my head, Magdalen?

3. Erhebung (Elevation)
Poem by Richard Dehmel

Give me your hand, only a finger, then I will see this entire globe as my property! Oh, how my country blossoms! Just take a look at it, so that it can accompany us over the clouds into the sun!

4. Waldsonne (Forest Sunshine)
Poem by Johannes Schlaf

Into the brown murmuring nights a light glitters, a greenish-golden glow. Flowers begin to gleam, and grasses, and the singing, leaping forest brooks, and memories. All your happy songs that died away long ago awaken once more, shining like gold. And I see your golden hair shining, and I see your golden eyes shining, out of the green, whispering nights. And I seem to be lying next to you on the grass and hearing you once more playing on the sparklingly bright panpipe into the blue air of heaven. Into the brown, gnawing nights a light glitters, a golden glow.

Six Songs
Op. 3 (1899–1903)

1. Wie Georg von Frundsberg von sich selber sang
(How Georg von Frundsberg sang about himself)
Poem from the folk collection Des Knaben Wunderhorn (The Boy's Magic Horn)

I have never spared my diligence and efforts, and have always looked after my lord; I accommodated myself to his best interests and hoped for his grace and favor, but attitudes at court often change. The man who sells himself advances beyond the rest and rises in life, but the man who long strives after honors must go far away from there; that vexes me greatly, my faithful service goes unrecognized. I receive no thanks or reward for it, they give me short weight and have altogether forgotten me; to be sure, I have endured great distress, danger—what pleasure shall I take in that?

2. Die Aufgeregten (The Excited Ones)
Poem by Gottfried Keller

What deeply agitated little life histories, what passion, what wild sorrow! A brook's wavelet and a little heap of sand broke each other's heart! A bee gave a muffled buzz and thrust its sting into a rose's fragrance, and a pretty butterfly tore its blue coat in the storm of a May breeze! And the flower closed its little sanctuary, dying because of the dew that was splashed away! What deeply agitated little life histories, what passion, what wild sorrow!

3. Warnung (Warning)
Poem by Richard Dehmel

You, my dog merely growled at you, and I poisoned him; and I hate anyone who creates discord. I am sending you two blood-red carnations, you my blood; on one of them is a bud. Care for all three, you, until I come. I will come not later than tonight; be alone, be alone, you! Yesterday when I arrived, you were staring into the sunset glow with someone! You: think about my dog!

4. Hochzeitslied (Wedding Song)
Danish poem by Jens Peter Jacobsen; German translation by Robert Franz Arnold

Never before has life woven such a full, rich wreath for the two of you, and the brightness of hope plays on the grapes in a gold gleam. Amid the leaves, what a glow of colorful sap, and how clearly the sounds flow together! Seize all of this, accomplish it, experience it in pleasure! The conquering power of youth boils in the fiery power of your blood; the fresh sap yearns for action, for the creativity of a free spirit. So, then, stretch the impetuous bows of your world, raise the slender columns up to the canopy of the sky; feel the new world with the heart's billowing flames!

5. Geübtes Herz (Experienced Heart)
Poem by Gottfried Keller

Do not turn away my simple heart because it has already loved so much! It is like a fiddle that a virtuoso has long played upon in pleasure and pain. And the longer he has played on it, the more its value rises to the utmost; for it produces with unerring force the melody that a skilled master elicits from its strings. Thus many a skilled woman has played true soulfulness into my heart. Now it is worthy of recommendation to you; do not pass by this valuable acquisition.

6. Freihold
Poem by Hermann Lingg

As many ravens as fly up at night, so many enemies are upon me; as many hearts as cling to other hearts, so many hearts flee from me. I stand alone, yes, all alone, like a dark stone by the roadside. But the stone is useful as a marker, watching over human activities: so that even the strong man will let the weak man enjoy his property in peace. The stone defies wind and rain, indestructible and alone. So then, I too will achieve my goal, prevent injustice until it collapses. Even if envy is lavish with its venom, I shall not succumb to it; lightning-flashes, inscribe on the stone: "If you want to be free, travel alone!"

Eight Songs
Op. 6 (1903–5)

1. Traumleben (Dream Life)
Poem by Julius Hart

An arm white as blossom encircles my neck. A young, warm springtime rests on my lips. I go about as if dreaming, as if my eyes were veiled. You have filled my entire world with your love. The world seems totally dead; there is only the two of us, with nightingales singing around us, in the blossoming rose grove.

2. Alles (Everything)
Poem by Richard Dehmel

Let us still wait for the night, until we see all the stars. Fold your hands; on the hard paths through the silent garden homesickness goes on tiptoe. It goes and fetches the anemone that you once pressed to your heart, it goes accompanied by the sound of that tree long ago from the top of which you picked your first longing for faraway places. And you shake out of your hair whatever gnaws at your soul, blessed child of thirty years; you have yet to learn everything, everything that is good for you.

3. Mädchenlied (Girl's Song)
Poem by Paul Remer

Oh, if Mother only knew how wildly you kissed me, she would pray endlessly for the Lord God to avert the calamity. And if my brother knew how wildly you kissed me, he would surely hasten as fast as the wind and kill you on the spot. But if my sister knew how wildly you kissed me, her heart, too, would beat longingly and would gladly endure happiness and sin.

4. Verlassen (Forsaken)
Poem by Hermann Conradi

At daybreak I left—fog lay in the streets . . . My heart was withered in torment—my lips spoke no word of farewell—they only moaned quietly: "Forsaken! Forsaken!" Do you know that torturing word? It gnaws like infamous shame! My heart was withered in torment—At daybreak I departed—out into the twilight regions! Toward the young May day: that was a strange match! Little by little the world now awoke. What was the splendid spring day to me? I only moaned quietly: "Forsaken!"

5. **Ghasel (Ghazel)** [an Arabic/Persian poetic form]
Poem by Gottfried Keller

I hold you in my arms, you hold the rose gently, and the rose holds a young bee within it. Thus we are strung like beads on one string of life, thus we are happy just as petal on petal joins together in the rose. And when my kiss glows on your lips, the trace of the flames thrills all the way to the bee's heart, which is paired with the heart of the rose.

6. **Am Wegrand (At the Roadside)**
Poem by John Henry Mackay

A thousand people pass by, the man I long for is not among them! Without repose my glances fly that way, they ask the hastening man whether he is the one . . . But they ask and ask in vain. No one replies: "Here I am. Be tranquil." Yearning fills up the confines of life, which fulfillment fails to fill, and so I stand at the roadside-beach while the multitude flows by until, blinded by the sun's blaze, my weary eyes close.

7. **Lockung (Allurement)**
Poem by Kurt Aram

Come, come along, just a step! I've already eaten, I won't gobble you up, come, come along, just a step! Come, come along, one more step! There is barely two toes' length still to go to reach the little house, come, my little mouse, oh, just look, we're there! Here in the little corner, pst (halt), don't be afraid, how your little cheeks are burning, now no screaming will help, you are mine, mine!

8. **Der Wanderer (The Journeyer)**
Poem by Friedrich Nietzsche

A journeyer walks through the night at a good pace; and crooked valleys and long hills—he takes them in his stride. The night is beautiful—he keeps walking and does not halt; he does not know where his path will take him. Then a bird sings in the night. "Ah, bird, what have you done? Why are you blocking my mind and my feet, and pouring sweet vexation of the heart into my ear, so that I must stand still and listen—why are you luring me with music and greetings?" The good bird stops singing and says: "No, journeyer, no! I am not luring *you* with my music. I am luring a female from the hills—what is that to you? When I am alone the night is not beautiful for me—what is that to you? For you must walk and never, never halt! Why are you still standing there? What did my flute song do to you, you journeyer?" The good bird fell silent and thought: "What did my flute song do to him? Why is he still standing there? The poor, poor journeyer!"

Six Orchestral Songs
Op. 8 (1903–5)

1. **Natur (Nature)**
Poem by Heinrich Hart

Night flows into day and day into night, the brook into the river, the river into the sea; life's splendor dissolves into death and death begets bright and noble life. And every spirit that strives ardently forces itself like a fountain into the whole world. What you are experiencing, I have experienced; what is illuminating me, has illuminated you. We are all parts of one tree, whether bough or twig or pith or leaf. Nature loves us all equally, she, the resting place of us all.

2. Das Wappenschild (The Coat of Arms)
Pamphlet text from Des Knaben Wunderhorn (The Boy's Magic Horn)

Storm, tear and rage, you winds of misfortune, show your full tyranny; shatter, smash branches as well as bark and rip in two the tree of hope; this hailstorm strikes the trunk and leaves, the root remains until storm and rain allay their fury, so that it puts forth green leaves and boughs again. My heart is not inferior to any diamond, my spirit is barely less firm than an oak; even if earth and heaven banished me, I would still defy the privation. Fall away, false friends; strike, bitter enemies; my heroic courage cannot be subdued; therefore I will fight and see what miracles patience performs. Love offers me a wine for bravery from golden goblets, promises to give me good pay, and leads me courageously into battle; there I will be victorious, here I will wage war; a green field serves my shield as a coat of arms, in which a palm tree lifts two anchors [*symbols of endurance and hope*].

3. Sehnsucht (Longing)
Poem from Des Knaben Wunderhorn

My days are heavy and dull since I departed from you, my treasure and highest joy, I realize that I must suffer; alas for the delay, it is too long, in my sorrow it is too long for me, so that I often lament, no day appears, no day appears, I think about this in my heart.

4. "Nie ward ich, Herrin müd" ("I have never grown tired, Lady")
Text based on a sonnet by Petrarch; German translation by Karl Förster

I have never grown tired, Lady, of being your loving servant, nor will I as long as my life lasts; but now I am being driven ashore through hatred of myself, and the endless flowing of tears makes me powerless. I would rather obtain a beautiful white grave than have your name inscribed on marble to my shame, when my spirit is separated from my body, (my spirit) which has now long dwelt within it. Therefore, if a heart experienced in love and fidelity suffice for you without preparing torments for it, let it receive your mercy. If your anger intends to conquer in another way, it is mistaken and will never get to see its purpose; for this, Love, I thank myself and your direction!

5. "Voll jener Süße" ("Full of that sweetness")
Text based on a sonnet by Petrarch; German translation by Karl Förster

Full of that sweetness, which—inexpressible—my eyes received from that beautiful face on the day when I would have preferred to go blind in order never to look upon lesser beauty, I abandoned what I loved best; and in rapture the gaze of my spirit is totally engrossed in her, (my spirit) which, as if from long habit, hates and looks down upon all that is not she. In a valley, enclosed all around, which grants cool relief to my weary sighs, I came slowly, meditating on love, to the spot; there I saw not women but rocks and fountains and the image of that day, (the image) which my spirit persistently paints for me wherever I turn my eyes.

6. "Wenn Vöglein klagen" ("When birds lament")
Text based on a sonnet by Petrarch; German translation by Karl Förster

When birds lament and amid green branches summer breezes tremble with a gentle rustling, when bright waves rise with a muffled murmur and play about flowery, fresh banks, I sit and write, devoted to love, and the woman whom heaven deigned to show us and whom the earth covered I then see still alive and graciously inclining toward my sighs from far away. "Why, alas, do you let yourself bleed to death prematurely?" she says, full of sympathy. "Why do you shed sorrowful streams from your sad eyes? Do not lament over me, I died in order to enjoy an eternal existence, and I opened my eyes in eternal blazes when I seemed to be closing them."

Das Buch der hängenden Gärten
(The Book of the Hanging Gardens)
Op. 15 (1908–9)

Fifteen Songs on Texts of Stefan George

I. Under the protection of dense clusters of leaves where delicate flakes snow down from stars, gentle voices proclaim their sorrows, fabulous animals spew streams from their brown maws into the marble basins from which the little brooks hasten away lamentingly: there came tapers to ignite the bushes, white forms to part the waters.

II. Grove in these paradises alternates with flowery meadows, pavilions, brightly painted flagstones. Slender storks' bills ripple ponds that gleam with fish, rows of birds in a dull glow trill on the oblique roof ridges and the golden sedges rustle—but my dream pursues only one thing.

III. As a novice I entered your enclosure; previously there was no amazement in my attitudes, no wish stirring in me before I caught sight of you. Look graciously upon the clasping of my young hands, choose me as one of those who serve you, and with merciful patience spare the one who is still stumbling on such an unfamiliar path.

IV. Since my lips are immobile and burn, I begin to observe where my feet have come to: into the splendid domain of other masters. It was perhaps still possible to break away, but then it seemed as if through high gate rails the glance before which I knelt untiringly was seeking me questioningly or was giving signs.

V. Tell me on which path she will walk by today, so that I can fetch soft silk weaves from the richest chest, can pick roses and violets, so that I can lay down my cheeks as a footstool beneath her soles.

VI. I am henceforth dead to all efforts. To call you near me with my senses, to spin out new conversations with you, service and payment, permission and prohibition, of all things only this is necessary, and to weep because the images that flourished in the beautiful darkness always vanish when the cold, clear morning threatens.

VII. Anxiety and hope oppress me in alternation, my words are prolonged into sighs, I am afflicted with such impetuous longing that I pay no heed to rest and sleep, that tears soak my bed, that I keep every joy away from me, that I desire no friend's comforting.

VIII. If I do not touch your body today, the thread of my soul will tear like a sinew that has been stretched too far. Let mourning crepes be beloved signs for me, who have been suffering since I have belonged to you. Judge whether I deserve such torment; sprinkle cool water on me, I am hot with fever and unsteadily leaning outside.

IX. Fortune is severe and obstinate with us; what could a brief kiss do? The fall of a raindrop on a parched, bleached desert, which swallows it without pleasure, which must do without new refreshment and which cracks open from new heat waves.

X. I contemplate the beautiful flowerbed as I tarry; it is enclosed by purpleblack thorn in which flower cups with speckled spurs tower, and velvetfeathered inclining ferns and fluffy-tufted flowers watery-green and round, and in the center bellflowers white and gentle—their moist mouth is of a fragrance like that of the sweet fruit from the fields of heaven.

XI. When behind the flowered gate, we finally felt only our own breathing, did we obtain the blisses we had imagined? I recall that we both began to tremble like weak reeds whenever we merely touched each other lightly, and that our eyes teared—you remained at my side a long time that way.

XII. Whenever, resting blissfully in deep meadows, we join our hands around our temples, veneration mitigates the burning of our limbs: and so, do not think about the misshapen shadows that rock up and down on the wall, (do) not (think) about the watchers who may separate us swiftly, and (do) not (reflect) that the white sand outside the city is ready to sip our warm blood.

XIII. You lean against a white willow by the bank; with the stiff points of your fan you protect your head as if with lightning bolts, and you roll your jewelry as if you were playing. I am in the boat which arches of foliage are guarding and which I invited you in vain to step into . . . I see the willows, which are bending lower, and flowers that are floating scattered on the water.

XIV. Do not always speak about the leaves, prey of the wind, about the shattering of ripe quinces, about the steps of the annihilators late in the year. About the trembling of the dragonflies in storms and (the trembling) of lights whose gleam is changeable.

XV. We peopled the evening-gloomy arbors, bright temples, path and flowerbed joyfully—she with smiling, I with whispering—Now it is true that she is going forever. Tall flowers pale or break, the glass of the pools grows pale and breaks, and I stumble in the decaying grass; palms jab with their pointy fingers. Unseen hands jerkily drive the hissing throng of withered leaves outside around the dun walls of the Eden. The night is cloudy and sultry.

Four Songs from *Gurrelieder* (Songs of Gurre)
(begun *ca.* 1901; completed 1911)

Danish text by Jens Peter Jacobsen; German version by Robert Franz Arnold

1. *Lied Waldemars:* "So tanzen die Engel"
(*Waldemar's Song:* "The angels do not dance")

The angels do not dance before the throne of God the way the world is now dancing before me. Their harps do not resound as lovingly as Waldemar's soul (does) for you. But, what is more, Christ did not sit next to God more proudly after the hard struggle for redemption then Waldemar now sits proudly and regally at Tovelille's side. Not more ardently do souls wish to find their way to the league of the blessed than I (sought) your kiss when I saw Gurre's battlements gleaming from Øresund. And I would not exchange their walls and the treasure they faithfully guard for Heaven's brightness and deafening sound and all the companies of the saints!

2. *Lied Toves:* "Nun sag ich dir zum ersten Mal"
(*Tove's Song:* "Now I say to you for the first time")

Now I say to you for the first time: "King Volmer [=Waldemar], I love you!" Now I kiss you for the first time, and put my arm around you. And if you say that I had already said so earlier and had ever bestowed my kiss on you, then I say: "The King is a fool who remembers fleeting trifles!" And if you say: "I probably am such a fool," then I say: "The King is right." But if you say: "No, I am not," then I say: "The King is bad."
For I kissed all my roses to death while I was thinking of you.

3. *Lied Waldemars:* "Du wunderliche Tove!"
(*Waldemar's Song:* "You strange Tove!")

You strange Tove! I am now so rich through you that I no longer own even a wish. My bosom is so light, my thoughts so clear, a wakeful peace lies over my soul.
There is such calm within me, such rare calm. Words remain on my lips ready to form bridges, but they sink back down to rest.
For I feel as if the pulse of your heart were beating in my breast, and as if my breast, Tove, were lifting your bosom.

And I see your thoughts arise and glide together like clouds meeting one another, and united they sway in changing shapes.

And my soul is calm; I look into your eyes and I am silent, you strange Tove.

4. Lied der Waldtaube (The Wood Dove's Song)

Doves of Gurre! Grief torments me, from the way here over the island! Come! Listen!

Tove is dead! Night (lies) upon her eyes, which were the King's daylight. Her heart is stilled, but the King's heart beats wildly, dead and yet wild! Strangely like a boat on the waves when the man, to receive whom the planks curved in homage, the ship's steersman, lies dead, tangled in the sea-weed of the depths. No one brings them news, the way is impassable.

Their thoughts were like two rivers, rivers flowing side by side. Where are Tove's thoughts flowing now? Those of the King wind along oddly, they seek for those of Tove, but do not find them.

I have flown far, I sought lamentation, I found much!

I saw the bier on the King's shoulders, Henning was supporting him; dark was the night, a single torch burned along the way; the Queen held it high on the balcony, her mind thirsting for vengeance. Tears that she did not want to shed sparkled in her eyes.

I have flown far, I sought lamentation, I found much!

I saw the King, he rode with the bier, in a peasant's doublet. His battle steed, which often bore him to victory, pulled the bier. The King's eyes stared wildly, searched for a glance! Strangely did the King's heart listen for a word. Henning spoke to the King, but he still kept on seeking word and glance. The King opened Tove's bier, stared and listened with trembling lips; Tove was mute!

I have flown far, I sought lamentation, I found much!

A monk wanted to pull the rope and ring an evening blessing; but he saw the driver of the carriage and heard the mournful news: the sun sank while the bell emitted funereal tones.

I have flown far, I sought lamentation and death!

It was Helwig's falcon that cruelly mangled Gurre's dove!

The Book of the Hanging Gardens

and Other Songs

To my teacher and friend Alexander von Zemlinsky

FOUR SONGS
Op. 2 (1899)

1. Erwartung *(Expectation)*

Poem by Richard Dehmel

Four Songs, Op. 2

2. Schenk mir deinen goldenen Kamm
(Give me your golden comb) (Jesus begs)

Poem by Richard Dehmel

From *Four Songs*, Op. 2 (1899)

3. Erhebung
(Elevation)

Poem by Richard Dehmel

From *Four Songs*, Op. 2 (1899)

Etwas bewegt (♩)

ausdrucksvoll

Gib mir dei - ne Hand, nur den Fin - ger, dann _____ seh ich die - sen gan - zen Erd - kreis als mein Ei - gen an!

beschleunigend

Oh, wie

SIX SONGS
Op. 3 (1899–1903)
1. Wie Georg von Frundsberg von sich selber sang
(How Georg von Frundsberg sang about himself)

Poem from the folk collection
Des Knaben Wunderhorn (The Boy's Magic Horn)

Etwas getragen (♩), kräftig

Mein Fleiß und Müh hab ich nie ge - spart und all - zeit ge-wahrt dem Herren

mein; zum Be - sten sein schickt ich mich

dan - nen weit, das sehr mich kränkt, mein treu-er

Dienst bleibt un - er - kennt.

p cresc.

Kein Dank noch Lohn da-von__ ich

ff

bring, man wiegt g'ring und hat mein gar ver-ges - -sen

2. Die Aufgeregten
(The Excited Ones)

Poem by Gottfried Keller

From *Six Songs,* Op. 3 (1899–1903)

Lyrics visible in the music:

Hei - lig - tüm - chen ster - bend ü - ber dem ver - spritz - ten Tau!

Breit, pathetisch

Wel - che tief - be - weg - ten Le - bens -

- läuf - chen, wel - che Lei - den - schaft, welch wil - der Schmerz!

sehr rasch und leicht

3. Warnung
(Warning)

Poem by Richard Dehmel

From *Six Songs,* Op. 3 (1899–1903)

4. Hochzeitslied
(Wedding Song)

Danish poem by Jens Peter Jacobsen
German translation by Robert Franz Arnold

From *Six Songs*, Op. 3 (1899–1903)

5. Geübtes Herz
(Experienced Heart)

Poem by Gottfried Keller

From *Six Songs*, Op. 3 (1899–1903)

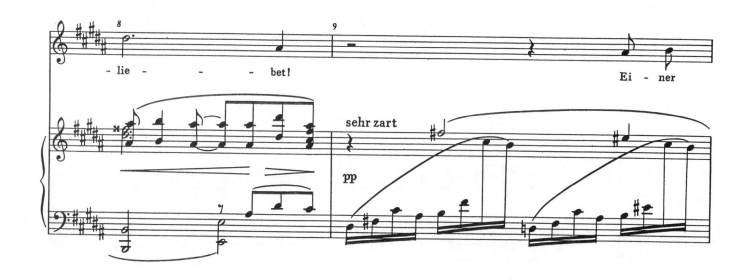

steigernd

Mei - ste - rin in mein Herz die rech - - te See - le.

Nun ist's wert, daß man es dir emp -

- feh - le, las - - - se nicht den köst - li - chen Ge -

- winn!

6. Freihold

Poem by Hermann Lingg

From *Six Songs,* Op. 3 (1899–1903)

Men - schen-tun: daß dem Schwachen auch der Star - ke laß das Sei - ne si - cher ruh'n.

Wind und Re - gen trotzt der Stein, un - zer - stör - bar und al - lein.

Wohl, so will auch ich voll - en - den,

Un - recht däm - men, bis es bricht. Mag sein Gift der

Neid ver-schwen-den, mich er - legt er nicht;

Blit - ze, schrei-bet auf den Stein: ____ „Wer will frei sein, geh' al -

rit.

- lein!"

EIGHT SONGS
Op. 6 (1903–5)
1. Traumleben
(Dream Life)

Poem by Julius Hart

Langsam, zart

Um mei - nen Na - cken schlingt sich ein blü - ten-wei - ßer

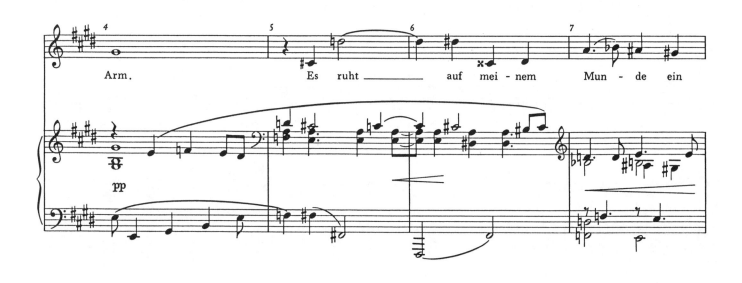

Arm. Es ruht _____ auf mei - nem Mun - de ein

Früh - ling jung — und warm. Ich wand - le wie im

Trau - me, als wär mein Aug ver - hüllt.

Du hast mit dei - ner Lie - - be

all mei - ne Welt er - füllt.

Die Welt scheint ganz ge - stor - ben, wir

bei - - de nur al - lein,

von Nach - - ti - galln um - klun - gen, im

blü - hen - den Ro - sen - hain.

2. Alles
(Everything)

Poem by Richard Dehmel

From *Eight Songs*, Op. 6 (1903–5)

Durchaus sehr zart, etwas langsam

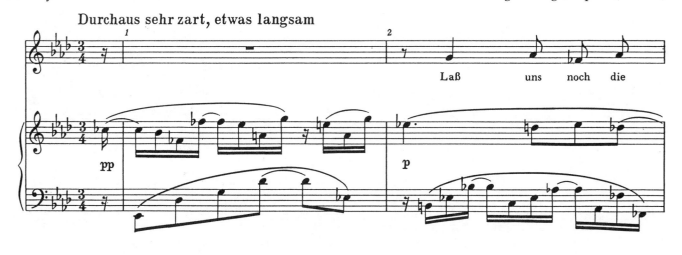

Laß uns noch die

Nacht er-war-ten, bis wir al-le Ster-ne sehn.

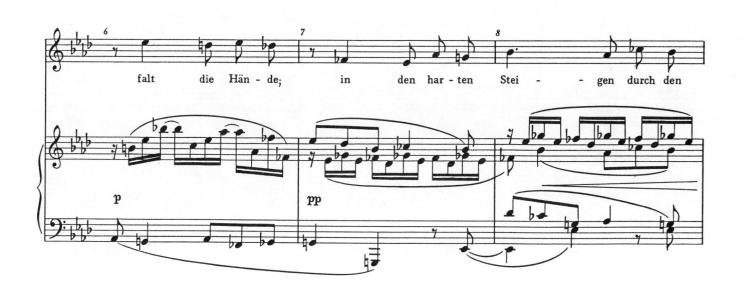

falt die Hän-de; in den har-ten Stei-gen durch den

3. Mädchenlied
(Girl's Song)

Poem by Paul Remer

From *Eight Songs*, Op. 6 (1903–5)

Sehr rasch

Ach, wenn es nun die Mut - ter wüßt', wie du so

wild mich hast ge - küßt,

sie wür - de

langsamer

be - ten oh - ne En - de, daß Gott der

steigernd

Herr das Un - glück wen - de.

4. Verlassen
(Forsaken)

Poem by Hermann Conradi

From *Eight Songs,* Op. 6 (1903–5)

Was war ___ mir der prangende Früh - lings-tag —

Ich stöhnte nur lei - se:

Ver - las - sen!...

5. Ghasel
(Ghazel*)

Poem by Gottfried Keller

From *Eight Songs*, Op. 6 (1903–5)

Mäßig, innig

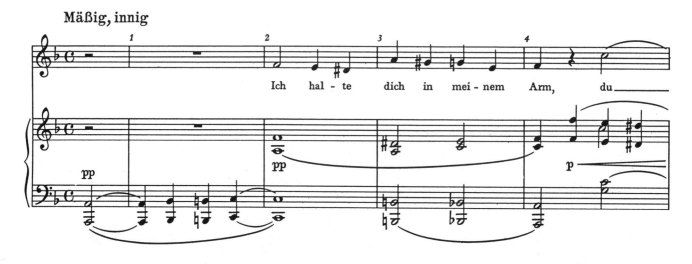

Ich hal-te dich in mei-nem Arm, du____

____hältst die Ro - se zart,____ und ei-ne

jun-ge Bie - - ne tief____ in sich die Ro - se hält.

*an Arabic/Persian poetic form

So rei - hen wir uns per - len - haft an ei - ner
Le - bens - schnur, so freun wir uns, wie Blatt an
Blatt sich an der Ro - se schart. Und glüht mein Kuß auf dei - nem

6. Am Wegrand
(At the Roadside)

Poem by John Henry Mackay

From *Eight Songs*, Op. 6 (1903–5)

Bewegt (♪)

Tau- -send Men- schen zie- hen vor- ü- - ber, den ich er- seh- ne, er

ist nicht da - bei! Ruh- - - los flie- gen die

Bli - cke hin - ü - ber, fra - gen den Ei - len- den, ob er es sei...

7. Lockung
(Allurement)

Poem by Kurt Aram

From *Eight Songs*, Op. 6 (1903–5)

Leicht, aber nicht allzu rasch

Komm, komm mit nur ei-nen Schritt!

Hab schon ge-ges- -sen, will dich nicht fres-sen, komm,

8. Der Wanderer
(The Journeyer)

Poem by Friedrich Nietzsche

From *Eight Songs,* Op. 6 (1903–5)

was hast du ge - macht! Was hemmst du mei - nen Sinn und Fuß und gie-ßest sü - ßen

Herz - ver - druß ins Ohr mir, daß ich ste - hen muß und lau - schen muß--

zurückhaltend

— was lockst du mich mit Ton und

Gruß?" Der gu - te Vo - gel schweigt

SIX ORCHESTRAL SONGS
Op. 8 (1903–5)

Arranged for piano & voice by Anton Webern

1. Natur
(Nature)

Poem by Heinrich Hart

lebt,   was mich   er - hellt,_____ hat   dich_____ er -

hellt.

All'   sind   wir   ei - - -

- - - nes   Baums_____ Ge - -

2. Das Wappenschild
(The Coat of Arms)

Pamphlet text from *Des Knaben Wunderhorn*
(The Boy's Magic Horn)

From *Six Orchestral Songs*, Op. 8 (1903–5)
Arranged by Anton Webern

und werft den Hoff - nungs-baum ent - zwei;

dies Ha - gel - wet-ter trifft Stamm und Blät - ter, die

Wur - zel bleibt, bis Sturm und Re - gen ihr

Wü - ten le - gen,

Etwas breiter.

doch dem Un - ge - mach;

weicht, fal - sche Freun - de, schlagt, bitt' - re Fein - de, mein Hel - den - mut ist

nicht_ zu dämp - fen;

drum will ich kämp - fen und sehn,_____ was die Ge - duld_____

für Wun - - der tut.

Lie - be schenkt aus gold - nen Scha - len mir ei - nen Wein zur Tap - - fer -

Die

3. Sehnsucht
(Longing)

Poem from *Des Knaben Wunderhorn*
(The Boy's Magic Horn)

From *Six Orchestral Songs*, Op. 8 (1903–5)
Arranged by Anton Webern

scheint___ kein   Tag,_____   des wird ge _ dacht___ im

Her _ _ _ zen.

4. "Nie ward ich, Herrin müd"

("I have never grown tired, Lady")

Text based on a sonnet by Petrarch
German translation by Karl Förster

From *Six Orchestral Songs*, Op. 8 (1903–5)
Arranged by Anton Webern

5. "Voll jener Süße"
("Full of that sweetness")

Text based on a sonnet by Petrarch
German translation by Karl Förster

From *Six Orchestral Songs*, Op. 8 (1903–5)
Arranged by Anton Webern

blind ich wär ge - gan-gen, um nim - mer klein're Schön - heit zu er -

blik - ken, ließ ich, was mir das

Liebst'; und mit Ent - zük - ken ist

ganz in ihr des Gei - stes Blick be - fan - gen,

der,   was   nicht   sie   ist,   wie   aus   ei - ner   lan-gen Ge-wohn - heit   haßt   und

an-sieht   mit   dem   Rük-ken.

steigernd

wieder breit

Sehr ruhig.

In ei - nem Ta - - le, rings um-her ver - schlos - sen, das mei-nen

mü - den Seuf - zern Küh - - lung spen - - - -

- det, kam lang - - sam, lie - - -

- be - sin - nend ___ ich zur Stel - - - le,

6. "Wenn Vöglein klagen"
("When birds lament")

Text based on a sonnet by Petrarch
German translation by Karl Förster

From *Six Orchestral Songs*, Op. 8 (1903–5)
Arranged by Anton Webern

DAS BUCH DER HÄNGENDEN GÄRTEN

(The Book of the Hanging Gardens)

Op. 15 (1908–9)

Fifteen Songs on Texts of Stefan George

I.

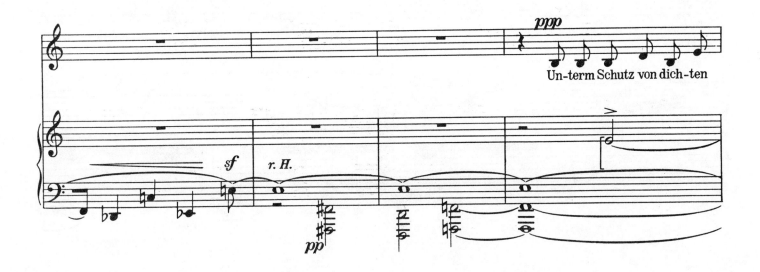

*) Die beigesetzten Metronomzahlen dürfen nicht wörtlich genommen werden, sondern sollen bloß die Zähleinheit (♩ ♩♪) des Grundtempos andeuten, aus welchem das Tempo frei zu gestalten ist.
Les chiffres de métronome indiqués ci-dessus ne devront pas être respectés avec exactitude. Ils ne donnent qu'une idée générale de la vitesse qui servira de base à un développement libre des „tempi".

The Book of the Hanging Gardens, Op. 15

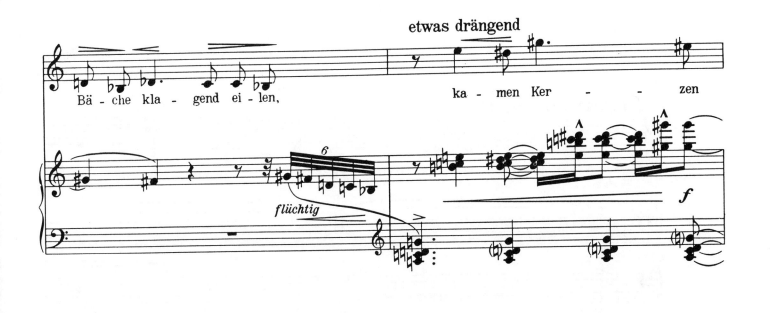

etwas drängend

Bä - che kla - gend ei - len,

ka - men Ker - - zen

wieder beruhigend

das Ge-sträuch ent - zün - den,

wei - ße For - men das Ge-

wäs - ser tei - len.

II.

Text by Stefan George

From *Das Buch der hängenden Gärten*
Op. 15 (1908–9)

III.

From *Das Buch der hängenden Gärten*
Op. 15 (1908–9)

IV.

Text by Stefan George

From *Das Buch der hängenden Gärten*
Op. 15 (1908–9)

Da mei - ne Lip - pen reg - los sind und bren - nen, be - acht ich erst, wo -

hin mein Fuß ge - riet: in an - drer

Her - ren präch - ti - ges Ge - biet.

V.

Text by Stefan George

From *Das Buch der hängenden Gärten*
Op. 15 (1908–9)

VI.

From *Das Buch der hängenden Gärten*
Op. 15 (1908–9)

VII.

Text by Stefan George

From *Das Buch der hängenden Gärten*
Op. 15 (1908–9)

Angst___ und Hof - fen wech - selnd mich be - klem - men,

mei - ne Wor - te sich in Seuf - zer deh - nen; mich be - drängt so

un - ge - stü - mes Seh - nen, daß ich mich an Rast und Schlaf nicht keh - re,

daß mein La - ger Trä - - - - - nen schwem - men, daß ich je - de

Sehr langsam
(♩ = ♪)

Freu - de von mir weh - - re, daß ich kei - nes Freundes

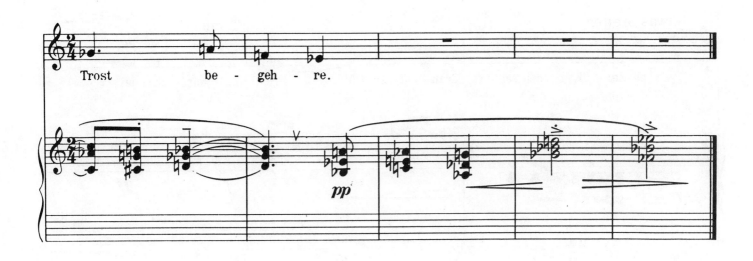

Trost be - geh - re.

VIII.

Text by Stefan George

From *Das Buch der hängenden Gärten*
Op. 15 (1908–9)

*) Immer die vorschlagende Sechzehntelnote stärker als den darauffolgenden Akkord.
La double croche d'agrément devra toujours être jouée plus fort que l'accord qui la suit.

IX.

Text by Stefan George

From *Das Buch der hängenden Gärten*
Op. 15 (1908–9)

X.

Text by Stefan George

From *Das Buch der hängenden Gärten*
Op. 15 (1908–9)

XI.

Text by Stefan George

From *Das Buch der hängenden Gärten*
Op. 15 (1908–9)

Als wir hin-ter dem be-blüm-ten To - re end - lich nur das eig-

XII.

Text by Stefan George

From *Das Buch der hängenden Gärten*
Op. 15 (1908–9)

XIII.

Text by Stefan George

From *Das Buch der hängenden Gärten*
Op. 15 (1908–9)

spiel - test dein Ge - schmei - de. Ich bin im Boot, das

Laub - ge - wöl - be wah - ren, in das ich dich ver - geb - lich lud zu stei - gen.....

die Wei - den seh' ich, die sich tie - fer nei - gen und Blu - men, die ver-

streut im Was - ser fah - ren. rit.

XIV.

Text by Stefan George

From *Das Buch der hängenden Gärten*
Op. 15 (1908–9)

XV.

Text by Stefan George

From *Das Buch der hängenden Gärten*
Op. 15 (1908–9)

Wir be - völ - ker - ten die a - bend - dü - stern

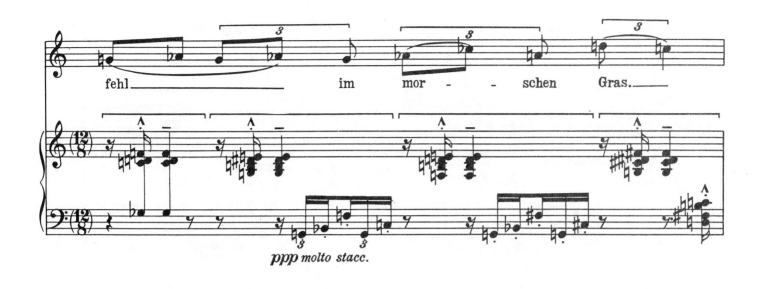

fehl_____ im mor - - schen Gras.____

ppp molto stacc.

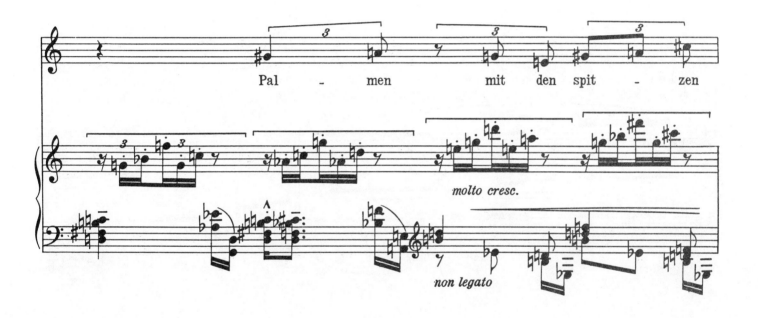

Pal - men mit den spit - zen

molto cresc.

non legato

molto rit. - - - - *etwas langsamer*

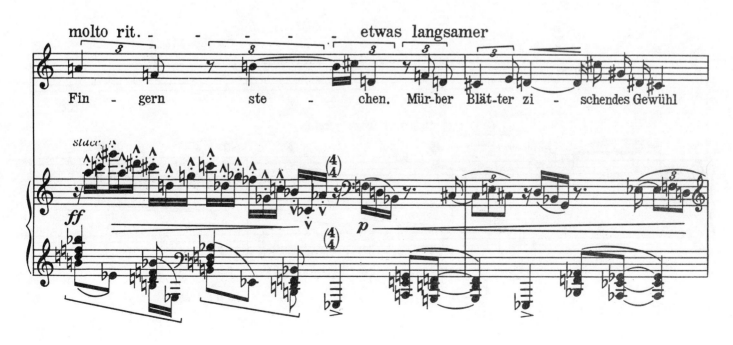

Fin - gern ste - chen. Mür-ber Blät-ter zi - schendes Gewühl

stacc.

ff

p

The Book of the Hanging Gardens, Op. 15

FOUR SONGS FROM *GURRELIEDER*

Danish text by Jens Peter Jacobsen; German version by Robert Franz Arnold

Arranged for piano & voice by Alban Berg

1. *Lied Waldemars:* "So tanzen die Engel"
(Waldemar's Song: "The angels do not dance")

2. *Lied Toves:* "Nun sag ich dir zum ersten Mal"
(Tove's Song: "Now I say to you for the first time")

Text: Jens Peter Jacobsen
German version: R. F. Arnold

From *Gurrelieder* (ca. 1901–11)
Arranged by Alban Berg

Four Songs from Gurrelieder

3. *Lied Waldemars:* "Du wunderliche Tove!"
(Waldemar's Song: "You strange Tove!")

Text: Jens Peter Jacobsen
German version: R. F. Arnold

From *Gurrelieder* (ca. 1901–11)
Arranged by Alban Berg

4. Lied der Waldtaube
(The Wood Dove's Song)

Text: Jens Peter Jacobsen
German version: R. F. Arnold

From *Gurrelieder* (*ca.* 1901–11)
Arranged by Alban Berg

glei - tend Seit' an Sei - te. Wo strö - men nun

To - ves Ge-dan - ken? Die des

Kö - nigs win-den sich selt - sam da-hin,

su - chen nach de - nen To - ves, rit. - - -

Four Songs from Gurrelieder

Four Songs from Gurrelieder

Wldt. Hel – wigs Fal – ke war's, der grau – – – sam

110

Wldt. Gur – res Tau – be zer – riß!

Etwas rascher.

111

782.24 S365

Schoenberg, Arnold,
1874-1951.
The book of the hanging
gardens : and other songs :
for voice and piano
Central Fine Arts CIRC
10/04

ifarw
Houston Public Library

Duckles 2/06